T. J. W. Pray

The reasons for modern alcoholic stimulation examined

.

T. J. W. Pray

The reasons for modern alcoholic stimulation examined

ISBN/EAN: 9783337717834

Printed in Europe, USA, Canada, Australia, Japan

Cover: Foto ©ninafisch / pixelio.de

More available books at **www.hansebooks.com**

MODERN STIMULATION, ETC.

BY

T. J. W. PRAY, M. D.

APPOINTED DEC., 1877, BY THE STRAFFORD DISTRICT MEDICAL
SOCIETY TO READ THIS PAPER BEFORE THE NEW HAMP-
SHIRE MEDICAL SOCIETY, IN JUNE, 1878.

CONCORD:
PRINTED BY THE REPUBLICAN PRESS ASSOCIATION.
1878.

THE REASONS FOR MODERN ALCOHOLIC STIMULATION EXAMINED.

BY T. J. W. PRAY, M. D., DOVER, N. H.

" *Tempora mutantur, et nos mutamur,*" etc., is an old Latin maxim, and in nothing is this better exemplified than in the different means used for the cure and treatment of disease. Change here is the order of the day. How different the medication of to-day and a hundred years ago ! The recommendations of the fathers are nearly all ignored, and the speculations of the present have full sway. What they did was imperfect, to say the least ; what we do, or theorize in, is progress,—advancement in science. And yet, in this desire for the novel, some truth which former ages recognized is often dressed up under a new guise and heralded forth as discovery. Much of the knowledge of idiopathic fevers and their laws is the result of former research. There is no question but that a great part of what has been written about the etiology of disease is merely theory, having no foundation in fact ; yet amid the rubbish of centuries, many a gem of truth gleams forth to enlighten and profit modern thought. Old medicines have been laid aside, and new ones have taken their place, perhaps no safer, nor of greater potency. We turn from the experience of other times with seeming distaste, so that we really have no medical literature in one department of our profession. Books printed from thirty to fifty years ago are old : the recent author is eagerly sought after. System after system, theory upon theory, have yielded to this desire for something different to avert pathological activity or remove pathological stimulation. The labors of learned minds, which have woven into the tangled web of subtle thought many an ingenious treatise, and revolutionized medical opinion, are set at nought. We own no man master, and no thought worthy of credence can stand for a moment unless fortified by more than mere assertion. And yet, as a profession, we have not arrived at a state of perfection. Much of the practice of to-day will be considered obsolete a hundred years hence. As long as disease cannot be cured, so long will different remedies be employed. We are not even independent actors. We are too much influenced by authority. We act in deference to the prejudices of others. Exigencies occur in the daily practice of the medical man, when he is controlled by the vague opinions of the non-medical world. Take, for instance, venesection. This remedy, although in use for over 2,000 years, has become unpopular, and is seldom employed. But we are not so far removed in point of excellence from the errors of our fathers. We also have fallen into extremes of practice, and follow after theories with like zeal. If they went beyond reason in the use of the lancet, we who live in glass houses should not throw stones. It has become the fashion—a fashion imported from Germany—to give enormous doses of quinine in typhoid fever to reduce the temperature of the body, as if this fever consisted only in the heightened heat of the system. Let us hope that its use in this manner may not lead to fatal complications. Along with this is the custom of giving alcoholic stimulants in large quantities, from the belief that disease is asthenic in character. When from eight to forty ounces of brandy, and even more, are prescribed in acute affections every twenty-four hours, some reason should be shown for such a course. In health, we should pronounce such a procedure to be pernicious and detrimental : why it is not so in disease has not been sufficiently explained. The usual apology for such a course is in the belief that the type of disease is changed. This influences the action of the physician at the bedside. As he believes, so will his therapeutics, in a great measure, be. If he supposes that debility reigns, it will lead to stimulation. If, on the contrary, a sthenic state is dominant, no recourse is had to such remedies. Now, is there any foundation for the supposition that there is a change in the type of discase? What is the opinion of medical men in this and other countries in regard to this question? Early in the present year, we addressed generally two inquiries to a few practitioners of medicine in this country, who have had from thirty-five to sixty years of experience, to ascertain their views and to find out the result of their observations upon this question, and the requirement of stimulation in the treatment of cases under their supervision. The following are extracts from this correspondence. We place the opinions of those who think there is a difference in type first, arranging them in the order of reception.

Dr. Hayes, the veteran editor of the *American Journal of Medical Science*, says,—" Since my entrance into the profession, now nearly sixty years, there has been a marked change in the type of disease from the sthenic to the asthenic. I have repeatedly, in the *Medical News and Library*, expressed this conviction."

Dr. E. T. Leonard, of Massachusetts: "I think for the last few years diseases are more asthenic, and require more stimulants and nourishment than formerly."

Prof. A. Smith, of this state (in a letter of Jan. 17, 1878), writes,—"I am very conscious of the change that has taken place in the type of disease, and if we would, the lancet could never be used again as in my earlier days. I began practice in 1833."

Dr. Wight, of this state: "I must answer, confidently, that there has been a change. Zymotic diseases are much more common than formerly; or, in other words, in my opinion, four fifths of the maladies we are called to treat at the present day, although having the external appearance of being inflammatory, are really asthenic in form. I believe the treatment in vogue fifty years ago would kill more patients now than it did then."

Dr. Dugas, of Augusta, Ga., writes,—"I must answer in the affirmative, that the type of disease has changed. As long ago as 1846 I observed a marked change in pneumonia, which prevailed epidemically in different parts of this state, and called the attention of my colleagues to it. Prior to this I had treated this disease by bleeding, tart. antimony, and other antiphlogistics; but now I found the type so changed that I could not bleed. I had to rely almost entirely upon quinine and opiates. In 1854 dysentery prevailed epidemically in different parts of the country, and the treatment by quinine was equally successful."

Dr. Woodward of Connecticut: "I do not hesitate to say that the type of disease has changed. Depleting remedies do not seem to be indicated as formerly."

Dr. Warner, of Connecticut: "I believe it is the general opinion of the older physicians, that diseases of the present time are of quite different type from those of thirty years ago. My impression is, that this is the universal opinion among the older practitioners."

Dr. Alfred C. Post, of New York city: "I have a very strong impression that active inflammatory diseases, characterized with a vigorous circulation, with a bounding, hard, and incompressible pulse, and requiring active depletion for their relief, are much less frequent than they were when I began my professional life; but I think the abandonment of depletion in the treatment of inflammation has been carried too far, and that there are still many cases of acute inflammatory diseases which can be controlled more efficiently, more speedily, and more safely by blood-letting and other depressive agents, than by the means which are now generally resorted to."

Dr. S. P. Smith, of Alabama, says,—"In 1837, when I commenced practice, all fevers were highly inflammatory, requiring blood-letting; but since 1849 fevers have changed, and require stimulants and feeding."

The following are the opinions of physicians who think there is no change in the human constitution or in the type of disease:

Dr. Ballou, of Rhode Island, writes,—"During my pupilage in medicine, and some few years afterwards, I regarded the fevers, and other diseases which fell under my observation, as far more sthenic than those which now, and for many years since, I have been called to treat. Fevers and other diseases, which occurred from 1828 to 1835, were more successfully treated by venesection, tarter-emetic, &c., than by tonics, stimulants, and what is now called a sustaining regimen."

Dr. Willard Parker, of New York city, says,—"It is now nearly fifty years since the profession began to talk of a change in the type of disease. Dr. Gallup, in Vermont, regarded every disease as *sthenic*, and requiring the lancet and tartarized antimony, while Drs. Miner and Tully, residing in Connecticut, believed every disease as *asthenic*, and relied on stimulants and opium. They were both representatives of extremes,—both right and both wrong,—Gallup's practice being safer in the country. I have failed to discover any change of type in disease : it is not an entity, but an action, and the action is modified by the patient's system."

Prof. Flint, of New York : "I have seen no reason to change the views, in relation to the matter of your inquiry, which I have expressed in my work on *Practice:* 'With a professional experience of nearly forty years, I do not hesitate to express the conviction that acute inflammations are essentially the same.' The opinion held by some, that such alterations (change of type) have occurred within the memory of those now living, does not rest on any solid basis."

Dr. Alonzo Clark, of New York : "I do not think there is any change in type. Such a change could only result from constitutional changes in all persons. That this has not occurred is evident in the fact that puerperal and accidental bleedings are just as well borne as they ever were ; and I believe that to-day the bleedings of Rush would do no more mischief than they did in his time."

Dr. C. Ellis, of Boston : "I have seen no change in the type of disease. I have never hesitated to feed and stimulate patients when they bore nourishment well and seemed feeble."

Prof. S. D. Gross, of Philadelphia : "From all I have seen of men, in health and disease. I have no reason to believe that the human constitution is at all different now from what it was when I entered the profession fifty years ago. I do not believe in a change of type in disease ; nor do I think that there is any more necessity for the use of stimulants in diseases and accident than there was formerly. If there is any change,—and I am sorry to say there is,—it is not in our patients, but in our modes of treatment, too often influenced by the authority of some great name or fashion in medicine."

Dr. H. I. Bowditch, of Boston : " I do not see any material difference in the type of disease as seen now and formerly."

Prof. N. S. Davis, of Chicago : " I do not think there has been any permanent change in the special type of diseases during the last half century, as supposed by many. Diseases of an epidemic and endemic character vary in severity, but no general change has been noted during the forty years I have been in practice."

Dr. T. H. Jewett, of South Berwick, Maine : " I have my doubts as to much change, as is generally stated, as to fevers, from the sthenic to the asthenic."

Prof. A. B. Palmer, of Ann Arbor, Michigan : " I do not think any general wide-spread change from the sthenic to the asthenic type of disease has occurred during the forty years I have been in the practice of medicine, and I do not believe stimulants are more required or better borne than forty years ago."

Dr. Phelps, of Windsor, Vt. : " To-day our fevers make a show of sthenicity quite formidable in the outset, but soon this condition gives way to asthenia, but on this account l am not prepared to say, pathologically speaking, that the type is changed."

Dr. William Perry, of Exeter, N. H., who has been in practice sixty-four years : " I have no doubt that there is ' change ' in the character of diseases, but there is quite as much difference in the brains of those who treat them. This is quite obvious from the starting-point, in regard to the nature of disease. Formerly any ache or pain had for its cause an inflammation, or, in the language of the day, a change of action, and the cure was in breaking it up. Neuralgia was hardly known, excepting the famous tic-douloureux. Bleeding does not often kill, and so it was constantly resorted to, to prepare the way for other remedies,—to change the action. This practice will often effect the object very promptly, and the doctor get credit for his skill. Now change the belief in the nature of disease, and believe it to depend on imperfect nervous influence, and we shall have asthenic form to perfection, which is not to be considered curable by venesection. Now these are somewhat the outlines to explain the change of sthenic to asthenic in the form of disease formerly and at the present time."

Dr. R. C. Hewitt, of Louisville, Ky. : " I have not observed nor do I believe any such change (from sthenic to asthenic) has taken place. The general characteristics of diseases now are just the same as they appeared to me thirty-four years ago. I do not believe stimulants are more necessary now than they were formerly."

Dr. Spofford, of Groveland, Mass., who has practised more than sixty-five years : " I do not think there is much change in the human constitution, but more in the manner of treatment of disease. I do not believe that bleeding can be laid aside to the extent it is, without costing some lives. In my early practice, at Hampstead, N. H., during a severe visitation of fever, stimulants were used freely with good results. In later years I have used less."

We could have extended these inquiries had we been better acquainted with the older physicians of the United States. Of course many letters have been unanswered, owing to sickness, and failure to reach those addressed.

In Europe, such men as Dr. Stokes, Sir Robert Christison, Allison, Graves, and others, affirm that there has been a change in the type of disease. Dr. Stokes speaks thus :

" Since the delivery of my address on ' Change of Type in Disease,' before the British Medical Association, at Leamington, in the year 1865, I have received numerous letters on the subject from leading physicians in England and Ireland. The testimony of these gentlemen has been of the strongest character, of the occurrence of an asthenic type of local inflammatory disease within forty years."*

This gentleman thinks the fathers of British medicine were correct ; that men, in forming their opinions, could not possibly have fallen into the practice of bleeding so largely, in the treatment of their patients, unless the maladies themselves called for such action ; that Sydenham, Haygarth, Fothergill, Heberden, Fordyce, Gregory, Cullen, Cheyne, and others, were men of giant minds, and could not have failed in their observations as to the true character of disease ; that their description of

---

* See Stokes's Lectures on Fever.

fevers is so different from what prevails now, as not to suppose that, in the early part of this century, they were sthenic in character ; that from his own knowledge, and of frequent occurrence, he noticed, in the epidemics of 1822 and 1828, the vehement action of the heart, the incompressibility of the pulse, the vivid redness of the venous blood, and the " force with which it spouted almost *per saltum* from the orifice of the vein." There was no call for stimulants then, but now, since asthenia reigns, they are required.

Of course this is high authority, and great respect must be shown to such opinions. Dr. Stokes, however, is not supported in his belief by all the leading minds of England. Prof. Bennett, Dr. Markham, and others, hold that the doctrine of the change of type is untenable.

Such is the state of medical opinion in this country and England upon this question. In the United States, many of the distinguished men of our profession, those who form medical opinion in the lecture-room, are unquestionably of the belief that there is no change in disease. While they maintain that venesection is called for now, in many cases, still it is required but occasionally, and should not be abused, as in the days of Rush.

Between these two conflicting views, which is the right one? Perhaps a solution to this question lies partly in considering what has been done in medicine for the last half century. There has been steady progress. New truths of vital importance have been discovered ; hygienic conditions are daily investigated ; physiology has become a more exact science ; chemistry has revealed valuable curatives, and made as clear as the light of noonday the great changes which disease produces in the body. The investigations going on in the domain of materia medica are revealing new properties to numerous medicinal agents. Pathological anatomy has familiarized us with the results of disease, which our fathers could only guess at. Our progress in this respect has been wonderful. A higher tribute is paid to the *vis medicatrix naturæ*. Less medicine is given, not because less is required, but in consequence of a better comprehension of its effects upon the system. The philosophical treatises of Dr. J. Bigelow of Boston, and Dr. Forbes of London, upon the efforts of nature in the sick-room, have solved many of its perplexities, and banished many false notions of what medicine can accomplish. For the last fifty years our treatment of disease has been greatly simplified, because we are sure that many diseases, as typhoid fever, rubeola, scarlatina, variola, etc., are self-limited, and not to be materially shortened in their course by any mode of treatment. The sick are often cured through nature's restorative powers, while the mind of the patient is quieted by the millionth part of a drop or grain of medicine.

If we treat diseased action differently from Sydenham, Cullen, and others, it is no disparagement to them to say that we, their sons, know as much, and ought (to keep up with the constant progress in every department of science) to be better informed as to the exact nature of sickness, and consequently treat it differently. It would be a reflection upon our profession, if disease were not less fatal and its progress less violent.

We can more easily control diseased action, lessen the severity of its onset, and make it milder throughout its course. In many instances certainty takes the place of doubt. A want has been filled, which had long been felt in practice, by such remedies as aconite, veratrum viride, potassium compounds, chloral, etc. To-day, if we would, we could not deal out the remedies as they did of "olden time." Study and research have given us advanced ideas; and we stand upon a more elevated plane, with more means at our command to battle with disease. Some ailments known to the ancients have been driven off the earth. It is not too much to expect that many others now seen, will, in the future, be heard of only in history.

Disease, then, has been modified by the intelligent action of our profession; but to say there is change in its type, implies that there are constitutional changes in all persons. It cannot be affirmed that we have deteriorated in any respect as a people in bodily force. In the war of the rebellion, soldiers, North and South, performed marches, suffered deprivations, and endured hardships, that would have thrown into the shade those of Cæsar, Hannibal, and Napoleon Bonaparte. Fatigue was not a prominent complaint. The farmer, mechanic, and day-laborer, in city, town, and country, are just as capable of meeting their wonted tasks as those of a century ago. Our young men and old are not bowed down by feebleness, nor by the entailment of constitutional weakness. The cares of business, the constant wear and tear of body and mind, do not make greater inroads upon the health. Besides puerperal and accidental hemorrhages, capital operations in surgery are just as well borne to-day as they ever were. We are not a nation of invalids. We have as strong men, healthy men, as ever walked the earth; and there is no evidence of decay in muscular power or endurance. Sickness has not increased;—in fact, the average length of life has lengthened.

If there is a change in type, when, and in what diseases is it found? Small-pox, typhus fever, dysentery, measles, diphtheria, and the like, always remain the same as to their essential characters, only qualified by depraved conditions of the system. Certainly this change is not in phthisis pulmonalis, for this is no more virulent: its subjects live as long and bear up as well against its insidious encroachments. There is no asthenic condition of the system here more than formerly, and the disease has not been on the increase. Nor do the diseases of the nervous system predominate over former years;—and yet the assertion is confidently made, that there has been a progression in the number of these diseases. Statistics do not sustain this view. To the question put to Dr. Roberts Bartholow, in a paper read before the International Medical Congress in 1877, Do conditions of modern life favor specially the development of nervous diseases? he was forced to reply in the negative. Dr. Althaus, of London, says the rate of deaths from these diseases does not appear to vary perceptibly from time to time, being about twelve per cent. of the entire mortality from all diseases; and he further says, that "nervous diseases are not, as is commonly asserted, more frequent, but on the contrary less numerous, in large towns than in the country." He gives the following statement in support of this: that the death-rate of London from nervous diseases was 10.66 per cent., while in southern England it was 11.20 per cent., and in Wales, 15.38 per cent.

But it is maintained, that in fevers there is much less force in

the circulatory system, and more debility generally, than were
described by authors fifty years ago ; that patients could not now
bear venesection, and would sink into a hopeless condition under such treatment. No one doubts that bleeding was abused
formerly by nearly every medical man. Then old men of eighty
years, and even infants of not more than two months, were
bled. It was used remorselessly in almost every complaint,—
in hemorrhages, in puerperal fevers, in injuries, even in erup-
tive fevers and anæmia. Immense quantities of blood were
drawn, and the operation repeated frequently a dozen times,
until the blood ceased to flow. The champions of this practice acted under a theory. It was the fashion for all to bleed.
Hardly any one stopped to question its utility. That it was
demanded in many instances, we have no reason to question :
that it could be borne even now, as recklessly employed as then,
there is not much doubt. Patients sank then, and they would
at the present time. Death followed too often the path of such
notions. All the excuse for such action lies in the supposition
that, in their limited acquaintance with therapeutical agents,
they had not means vigorously to combat otherwise inflammatory action. It was the excess in bleeding which was repre-
hensible, and brought it into disfavor. There were times then,
as now, when its employment offered such relief as nothing else
could. The recent testimony of Prof. Clark, Drs. Post, Flint,
and Parker, together with Fordyce and Barker of New York,
and Gross of Philadelphia, with many others, all goes to
show that the modern abandonment of venesection has been
fraught with evil and the sacrifice of life ; that it is a remedy where aconite, veratrum viride, and other vital depress-
ants, cannot meet the conditions of many acute and chronic
diseases.

But it is asserted that modern forms of sickness are
quite often asthenic. This is no doubt the truth. It has
always been thus. The same diseases change from year to
year in mildness and severity. Epidemic and endemic com-
plaints vary in the degree and course of their sthenic and
asthenic character, and differ in one locality from another ac-
cording to the difference in the local sanitary conditions. This
has been recognized by every careful observer. It is the

law of disease. Sydenham, in his day, remarked upon this phenomenon. Diseases mild and severe go and return, bearing all the characteristics of former years, only qualified by certain surrounding influences. Typhoid fever often loses its typical symptoms. The brown tongue, sordes, epistaxis, and numerous other concomitants of this affection, are seen and not seen, and yet the disease is typhoid in character and continuance. These varying appearances may be due to the exciting cause being less violent, to hereditary tendency in the constitution, to life in populated places, to season, climate, earliness of treatment, stage, extent of disease, and to the artificial habits of society. The man of the country, inured to toil, with the robustness gained in the invigorating atmosphere of New England, is more likely to have disease sthenic in form, and consequently bear a more vigorous treatment, than the one environed by the effeminate influences and impure atmosphere of city life. Let the two exchange situations, and a change at once occurs. Then there is difference in constitution. No two examples will exhibit the same characteristics throughout, and they will not admit of precisely the same remedies. What will do for one patient may not work well for another. We shall never find a universal panacea that will apply to any one disease. There is scarcely a malady which does not admit of a variety of management. Hufeland has indicated the true way of meeting the requirements of the sick-room, namely, " to generalize the disease and individualize the patient." Even the trusting to statistics, valuable as they are, will rob each case of its true individuality. He who follows stimulation as an invariable line of treatment is a routinist, and prescribes for a mere name, and not for the case he is called to treat.

Dr. Todd, of England, and his followers, believe that disease has become asthenic. Accordingly excessive stimulation is recommended in almost every case. This system admits of no half-way measures: if patients are not held up by alcoholic preparations, they will certainly die. Now this is a mere theory, as much so as Brown's, or Brousais'. It conceives of conditions not occurring in actual life. It makes assumptions that do not warrant its entire reliability if carried into operation. It is not the truth, that stimulants will do most for the sick.

Take, for instance, pneumonia, as a representative disease. It has been variously treated. There is the *expectant* plan, which gives little or no medicine: here, one in three die. Homœopathy gives like fatality. In Dr. Todd's stimulant method, one in nine dies; in the restorative course of Dr. Bennett and others, one in thirty-two dies. Doubtless the same results would be found if statistics were examined as to other diseases. Now no one can question the ability of Dr. Todd as a writer and clinical lecturer, but either he met with patients not usually observed in ordinary practice, or he was wedded to wrong notions of what is actually occurring in the human constitution. Dr. Gross remarks upon this point,—" Dr. Todd was an able man, but that he was a profound thinker I doubt; and it is well to bear in mind that the patients at King's College Hospital, London, of which he had charge, were persons in the lowest walks of life, broken down by privation and various forms of intemperance, and therefore unable to bear depleting remedies. Such patients as Dr. Todd had are to be found in the wards of every elemosynary institution of Europe and this country. It was from the study of this class of cases that he deduced the doctrine of change in the character of disease." From the spread of his writings and opinions we have lost sight of much judicious treatment. Alterative medicines are quite often discarded. Cathartics weaken too much, in the judgment of this class of thinkers. Nervines, depressor motors, and stimulants constitute the great bulk of their recommendations for the sick. Now none can deny that stimulation in many acute inflammations is positively hurtful. It does not control, but, rather, increases the severity of symptoms. Whenever taken into the stomach, alcohol increases its vascularity, and tends after a short time to weaken its tone. If it be desirable to sustain the strength of the patient, then our aim should be not to injure the vitality of this organ. Large quantities of alcoholic mixtures produce catarrah of the stomach, upset its normal action, and interfere with the digestive process. Why, then, are such large quantities given? To keep up the heart's action, say some : to maintain the strength, say others: to prepare the patient to pass over a crisis; to conserve the vital powers, and prevent too much waste of the body ; to lessen the heat ; to quiet the nervous system by its anodyne qualities; and as a food or a sedative, say many. These are some of the reasons why stimulants are given, and yet almost every one of these suppositive properties are questioned. For a majority of them we have medicines of undisputed action, that will as surely meet these various conditions. Besides, many think that the administration of stimulants tends to injurious results in disease. Dr. Gross says that " whiskey and brandy kill as many people at the present day, as the lancet and tartar-emetic did in former times." Dr. Hewitt writes,—"I feel sure that the free use of stimulants in disease, which prevails now, results in the aggregate in vastly more injury than good." Prof. Palmer writes,— " I would retain it [alcohol] in the materia medica, but its utility is far more restricted than most of our medical literature seems to indicate, and its evils as a medicine strictly are far greater. Its use, with persons in health or in the ordinary conditions of debility, is more than an absurdity. It is, as Napoleon would have said, worse than a crime ; it is a blunder." Dr. Alonzo Clark, in his recent lectures on typhoid fevers, says,— "As a matter of fact, two thirds of the patients sick with this malady do better without than with alcoholic stimulants." Dr. Willard Parker believes in the stimulant effects of alcohol as an effort of nature to throw off an offending substance. He regards it as an irritant,—as much so as a grain of sand forced into the eye.

We would, then, class the wholesale manner of giving brandy, etc., to the sick, as it is often done, in the same catagory of extreme and radical measures as the use of the lancet sixty years ago ; as the tartar-emetic treatment of Rasori, or the blue pill of Abernethy. It is a one-idea medication, not broad, or comprehensive.

But let us not be understood as discarding the use of alcohol altogether. Its abuse we deprecate. If resort be had to it, it should be given in conjunction with food, with milk or farinaceous preparations, so that assimilation in debilitated conditions of the stomach may be secured. "It is necessary to insist on this point," says Ringer, "as it is common with both medical men and the laity to trust to alcohol alone, forgetting that while it benefits by stimulating the heart, it also effectually aids the digestive process, and this supports the patient in the best and most natural manner."

The rules laid down by Dr. Armstrong for the use of alcoholic mixtures are,—If the tongue becomes moist, the pulse slower, the skin not dry, the breathing tranquil, or if they produce sleep, then they do good. If, on the contrary, the tongue becomes dry and baked, the pulse quickens, the skin hot and parched, and the breathing hurried, they do harm. Dr. Stokes would administer them when the first sound and impulse of the heart over the left ventricle are enfeebled, and the first sound over the right ventricle is diminished, together with the marks of a depressed condition of the system. Dr. Bowditch says,—"I never prescribe whiskey or brandy, save with a limit as to the time of their use. I think physicians have done an immense injury by neglect of this obvious rule."

After all, our judgment is, if a patient is feeble, we have means far better than alcohol, and vastly more beneficial to the patient, and that is, in keeping up the strength of the patient by proper nourishment, judicious feeding, and suitable tonics. This gives satisfaction to physician and patient. In passing through the convalescent wards of the hospital over which Dr. Graves of England presided, some one remarked upon the healthy appearance of the convalescents. He replied,—" This is all owing to our good feeding. Will you, when the time comes, write my epitaph, and let it be, 'He fed fevers'?"